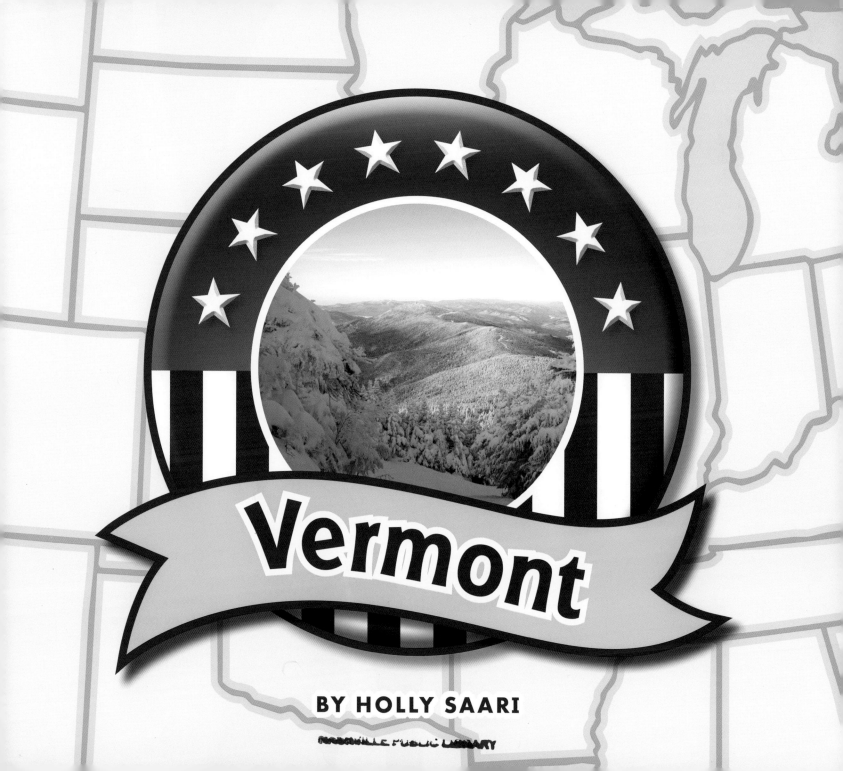

Vermont

BY HOLLY SAARI

The Child's World

Published by The Child's World®
1980 Lookout Drive • Mankato, MN 56003-1705
800-599-READ • www.childsworld.com

ACKNOWLEDGMENTS
The Child's World®: Mary Berendes, Publishing Director
The Design Lab: Design and production
Red Line Editorial: Editorial direction

PHOTO CREDITS: Marcio Jose Bastos Silva/Shutterstock Images, cover, 1, 3; Matt Kania/Map Hero, Inc., 4, 5; Photolibrary, 7; Liz Van Steenburgh/Shutterstock Images, 9; 123RF, 10; Jing Li/iStockphoto, 11; Jan Tyler/iStockphoto, 13; North Wind Picture Archives/Photolibrary, 15; Chris Ringenbach/iStockphoto, 17; Jeb Wallace-Brodeur/AP Images, 19; Barry Winiker/Photolibrary, 21; One Mile Up, 22; Quarter-dollar coin image from the United States Mint, 22

LIBRARY OF CONGRESS CATALOGING-IN-PUBLICATION DATA
Saari, Holly.
  Vermont / by Holly Saari.
     p. cm.
  Includes index.
  ISBN 978-1-60253-490-2 (library bound : alk. paper)
  1. Vermont—Juvenile literature. I. Title.

F49.3.S325 2010
974.3—dc22

2010019330

Printed in the United States of America in Mankato, Minnesota.
July 2010
F11538

On the cover: Vermont has snowy winters. Many people come to the state to ski.

CONTENTS

Geography

Let's explore Vermont! Vermont is in the northeastern United States. This area is called New England. Vermont shares its northern border with Canada.

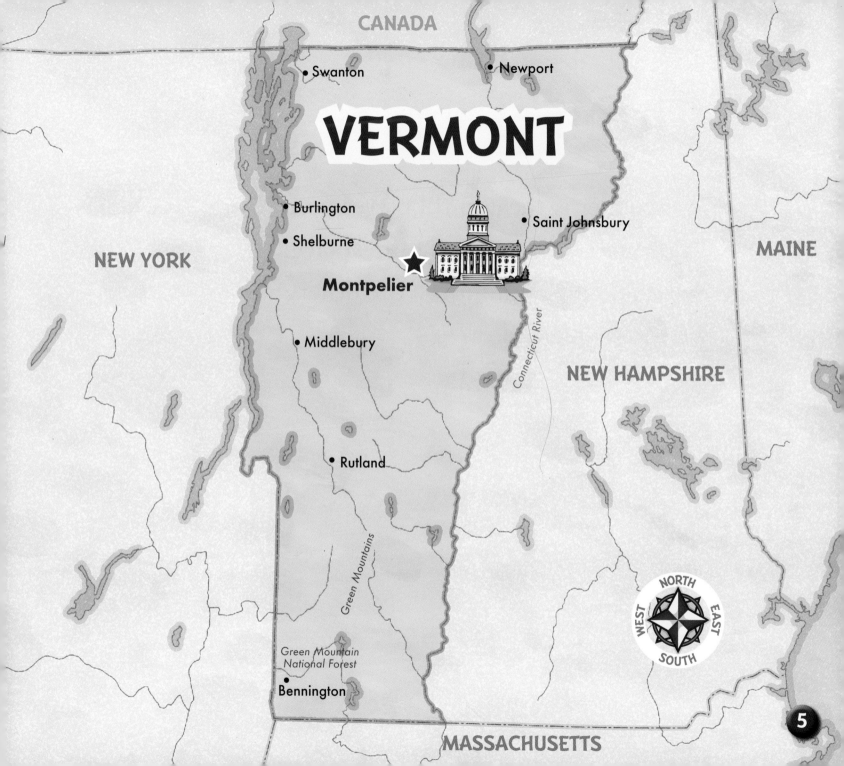

CANADA

• Swanton   • Newport

VERMONT

NEW YORK

• Burlington

• Shelburne   • Saint Johnsbury

Montpelier

MAINE

• Middlebury

NEW HAMPSHIRE

Connecticut River

• Rutland

Green Mountains

Green Mountain
National Forest

• Bennington

NORTH
WEST   EAST
SOUTH

MASSACHUSETTS

Cities

Montpelier is the capital of Vermont.
Burlington is Vermont's largest city.
Rutland and Bennington are other
well-known cities.

About 38,000 people live in Burlington. ▶

Land

Vermont is home to the Green Mountains. Valleys between the mountains make good farmland. Vermont's eastern border is the Connecticut River.

Vermont has more than 200 mountains that are taller than 2,000 feet (610 m).

Horses graze in the Green Mountains in Vermont. ▶

Plants and Animals

Most of Vermont is covered in forests. Many animals such as deer, bears, beavers, foxes, and rabbits live in these wooded areas. The state tree is the sugar maple. The state bird is the hermit thrush. It is a songbird. The state flower is the red clover.

Sugar maple trees turn beautiful colors in the fall. ▶

People and Work

About 620,000 people live in Vermont. Only Wyoming has fewer people. Most people in Vermont live in small towns or **rural** areas. Many of these people are dairy farmers. Apples are an important Vermont crop. Some people make things such as tools, machines, and **technology** products. Others work in mining or **tourism**.

A lot of maple syrup is made in Vermont. Maple syrup is made from the sap of sugar maple trees.

A man and a woman pick blueberries on a Vermont farm. ▶

History

Native Americans lived in this area long before settlers from Europe arrived. In the 1600s, people from France came to the Vermont area. In 1777, Vermont became an **independent** nation. It stayed this way for 14 years. Vermont joined the United States in 1791. It was the fourteenth state.

Vermont settlers traveled along the Connecticut River. ▶

Ways of Life

Many skiers travel to Vermont each year. Others come to see the state's nature and visit its small towns. Vermont is known for its **folk music**. The state holds music **festivals** throughout the year.

Some people go to Sugarbush, a resort in Vermont. There, they can ski and snowboard. ▶

Famous People

Former U.S. presidents Calvin Coolidge and Chester A. Arthur were born in Vermont. John Deere was also born in Vermont. He is known for making farming **equipment**. Author Katherine Paterson lives in Vermont. She wrote famous books such as *Bridge to Terabithia*.

Katherine Paterson has won awards for her books. ▶

Katherine Paterson was born in China in 1932.

Famous Places

Visitors to Sugarbush Farm in Vermont can see how maple syrup is made. They can also enjoy outdoor activities in Green Mountain National Forest.

Green Mountain National Forest has ▶ 900 miles (1448 km) of trails.

State Symbols

Seal

On Vermont's state seal, a cow and some grain stand for farming. A pine tree is in the center. Go to childsworld.com/links for a link to Vermont's state Web site, where you can get a firsthand look at the state seal.

Flag

Vermont's state flag has mountains and a tree to stand for nature.

Quarter

Vermont's state quarter shows a person getting sap from a maple tree. The quarter came out in 2001.

Glossary

equipment (ih-KWIP-munt): Equipment is the set of items needed to do something. John Deere made farming equipment.

festivals (FESS-tih-vulz): Festivals are celebrations for events or holidays. Vermont is known for its music festivals.

folk music (FOHK MYOO-zik): Folk music is the traditional music of an area. Vermont is known for its folk music.

independent (in-deh-PEN-dent): If an area is independent, it rules itself. Vermont was independent for 14 years.

motto (MOT-oh): A motto is a sentence that states what people stand for or believe. Vermont's state motto is "Freedom and Unity."

rural (ROOR-ul): Rural means having to do with the countryside. Many people in Vermont live in rural areas.

sap (SAP): Sap is the liquid inside a plant or tree. Maple syrup is made from the sap of maple trees.

seal (SEEL): A seal is a symbol a state uses for government business. Vermont's seal shows a cow and grain to stand for farming.

slavery (SLAYV-ur-ee): Slavery is the act of owning a person as property, forcing him or her to do work, and often treating that person badly. Vermont was the first state to make slavery against the law.

symbols (SIM-bulz): Symbols are pictures or things that stand for something else. The seal and the flag are Vermont's symbols.

technology (tek-NAWL-uh-jee): Technology is scientific knowledge applied to practical things. Some people in Vermont work to make technology products.

tourism (TOOR-ih-zum): Tourism is visiting another place (such as a state or country) for fun or the jobs that help these visitors. Tourism is popular in Vermont.

unity (YOU-nih-tee): Unity means being joined together. Unity is part of Vermont's state motto.

Further Information

Books

Keller, Laurie. *The Scrambled States of America*. New York: Henry Holt, 2002.

Reynolds, Cynthia Furlong. *M is for Maple Syrup: A Vermont Alphabet*. Chelsea, MI: Sleeping Bear Press, 2002.

Thornton, Brian. *The Everything Kids' States Book: Wind Your Way Across Our Great Nation*. Avon, MA: Adams Media, 2007.

Web Sites

Visit our Web site for links about Vermont: *childsworld.com/links*

Note to Parents, Teachers, and Librarians: We routinely verify our Web links to make sure they are safe and active sites. So encourage your readers to check them out!

Index